THE POWER
OF MONEY

BY DR. E. BERNARD JORDAN

ISBN 1-881787-01-X

This book is dedicated to:
Joshua Nathaniel Jordan
Who shall excel in his generation in
portraying the Kingdom of God

In Gratitude

We'd like to give the following individuals a special thank you for their faithfulness and support in helping to make our dream come true:

The Ministerial Board of Zoe
    Ministries
The Deacon Board of Zoe
    Ministries
The Deaconess Board of Zoe
    Ministries
Dolores Manning
    Complete Christian
    Women's Ministry
Elizabeth Sibeko

Avis & Gina Thompson
Georgina Anderson
Ministers Issaac & Deborah
    Jones
Anthony Prime
Ministers Devon & Faye
    Thompson
Deacon Cardon & Deaconess
    Aretha Pompey
Jean E. Harper

Because of their generosity and obedience to the Spirit of God, we know that they have opened the door for miracles, and we believe that He shall cause the gems of wisdom that are contained within these pages to be made manifest in each of their lives, for the reward of the Lord is sure, and addeth no sorrow! These are men and women of vision – the sons and daughters of Issachar...and they shall have knowledge of the times!

In His Love and Service,
DR. E. BERNARD & PROPHETESS DEBRA JORDAN

Table Of Contents

Chapter One
Wise Use of Money

"For the kingdom of heaven is as a man traveling into a far country, who called his own servants, and delivered unto them his goods.

And unto one he gave five talents, to another two, and to another one; to every man according to his several ability; and straightway took his journey.

Then he that had received the five talents went and traded with the same, and made them other five talents.

And likewise he that had received two, he also gained other two.

But he that had received one went and digged in the earth, and hid his lord's money.

After a long time the lord of those servants cometh, and reckoneth with them.

And so he that had received five talents came and brought the other five talents, saying, Lord, thou deliveredst unto me five talents; behold, I have gained beside them five talents more.

His lord said unto him. Well done, thou good and faithful servant; thou hast been faithful over a few things, I will make thee ruler over many things: enter thou into the joy of thy lord.

He also that had received two talents came and said, Lord, thou deliveredst unto me two talents: behold, I have gained two other talents beside them.

His lord said unto him, Well done, good and faithful servant; thou hast been faithful over a few things, I will make thee ruler over many things: enter thou into the joy of thy lord.

Then he which had received the one talent came and said, Lord, I knew thee that thou art a hard man, reaping where thou hast not sown, and gathering where thou hast not strewed:

And I was afraid, and went and hid thy talent in the earth: lo, there thou hast that is thine.

His lord answered and said unto him, Thou wicked and slothful servant, thou knewest that I reap where I sowed not, and gather where I have not strewed:

Thou oughtest therefore to have put my money to the exchangers, and then at my coming I should have received mine own with usury.

*Take therefore the talent from him, and give it
unto him which hath ten talents.*
*For unto every one that hath shall be given, and
he shall have abundance: but from him that hath
not shall be taken away even that which he hath."*

Matthew 25:14-29

God's purpose for placing financial substance into
your hands is to manifest increase in your life.
Contrary to the lie of popular opinion, God desires
every aspect of your life to prosper under His
blessing...including your money. In Jesus' parable of
the talents, the Lord became very upset with the
"wicked" servant on the day of reckoning because he
had dealt unwisely with his finances. Foolish
handling of the finances which have been entrusted
to you will corrupt the cycle of blessing and cause the
curse of poverty to embody your life. Most of the
time, we violate the principles of God through
ignorance, choosing to make financial decisions
according to what "seems right at the time." But
God's Word is immutable--it never changes or bends
to accommodate any of our reasonings and mental
gymnastics! It behooves us all to discover what God
has to say concerning finances. Jesus commanded us

Prophetic Principle #1

God wants you to prosper!

3

to "make friends with mammon" (Luke 16:9). God's plan is for us to understand the power of money and utilize it without becoming controlled by it.

You must first consider whose hands money is in to determine whether money is wicked or righteous. If you desire to experience the financial increase of God in your life, you must be diligent in your handling of the finances that God puts into your hands.

10 Key Wealth Principles
1. Wealth grows wherever men exert energy.
Wealth will always increase whenever your energy is focused in its direction. Maintaining focus means to keep your eyes fixed in the direction of your goal. Diffused vision will cause you to bypass the agenda,

Prophetic Principle #2

When money is working for you, it generates wealth.

and your energy will dissipate and nothing will be accomplished.

2. Opportunity wastes no time with the unprepared.
One must be prepared to greet opportunity when she presents herself. There is nothing more frustrating than to have a dynamic opportunity appear in your life, yet have your lack of preparation force you to decline the

offer. Too many people can recite the litany of missed opportunities because they weren't prepared financially, emotionally or educationally. Some people miss opportunity through their fear of success...and some through the fear of failure. Missed opportunities will plummet you to the depths of despair, and haunt you with the ghastly cries of "I could have..." or "I should have..."

3. Money is designed to work for you.

When money is working for you, it generates wealth. If you are working for money, then you are its slave. You might respond, "I am not a slave, I work for myself." However, many are in bondage to the routine of working without experiencing the reality of being gainfully employed. Their lifestyle never fully gains economic strength. "I owe, I owe, so off to work I go," speaks to your situation, then you are a slave at a higher level. For example, if you are earning $50,000 a year and your living expenses are $50,000 also, then you are serving money and money has become your master.

4. Money is designed to be your servant.

Prophetic Principle #3

You should tithe with the first 10 percent of your income.

5

Contrary to the notion of living paycheck to paycheck, God wants you to keep and invest a portion of your income so that it will circulate and serve you. You should be able to take a portion of whatever substance you receive and skillfully manage it so that it will bring increase into your life.

5. A part of everything that you earn is yours to keep.

A Savings Principle:

You should tithe with the first 10 percent of your income. The second 10 percent should be your offering. With the third 10 percent of your earnings, at the very least, you should pay yourself. This will enable you to activate that treasure to create more treasure in your bank account. It is God's desire for you to have money. Jesus did not teach against money, He taught us how to profit.

6. Wealth is not determined by the amount a man has in his hands, but by his ability to create more substance.

True wealth is not found in a stationery amount of money that is stashed away, for when that amount is depleted, how shall it be regained unless one has the ability to replace what was lost?

7. Wealth is reserved for those who understand its laws.

If you abuse the universal ethic and integrity of money, then you will offend it's character and cause money to flee from you rather than cleave to your presence.

8. **Money is currency and currency is designed to flow.**

When your money is not moving in a beneficial direction, you are abusing the purpose of money.

The master was grieved in the parable of the talents when, after entrusting his talents to each of his servants, one could not show a profit--he had hidden his money in the earth. The money became stagnant, lacked movement, and emitted a stench in his nostrils.

Are the talents and seeds of greatness on the inside of you moving or are they stagnant? In this hour, God is demanding movement! He demands that the currency we are blessed to oversee will become a force in the earth....a conductor of energy in order to fulfill its purpose.

Prophetic Principle #4

Money will escape the unskillful.

9. **Money works diligently for those who can apply it to profitable work.**

The ears of money are always attentive to the voice of one who understands its purpose. It is always willing to work when given something viable to perform. Money degenerates when left idle and will lose its energy and vitality. Work is merely the outgrowth of purpose, which money is compelled to fulfill.

7

10. **Money slips away from the unskillful who do not know how it should be guarded.**
    If you are unskillful concerning the laws of wealth, then money will escape you. Money will gravitate and bring increase towards those who possess wisdom. When the Lord came and saw what the other two servants had done with their talents He said, "Well done, good and faithful servant." Remember, the hand of the diligent shall be blessed, but those who deal with a slack hand shall always tend towards poverty.

How to Double Your Substance

The safest way to double your substance is by investing it in the banking institutions at a certain percent of interest. It is known as "The Rule of 72".

You must divide 72 by the rate of return. For instance, if the interest rate is 9 percent, then divide 72 by 9 percent. You will find that it will take eight years for your money to double at 9 percent interest.

Investing time is more valuable than investing money. Many of us do not have time to wait for our investments to mature because we live in an instant society. We want instant grits, oatmeal, and coffee. Whereas, in times past, it took two hours to cook a dinner, it now takes less than 30 minutes because of the the latest innovation, the microwave. We've become accustomed to instant gratification, and expect it in every strata. As a result of our lack of patience, we are not prepared for future financial challenges. We've been living in a devilish delusion! Some of us are depending upon Social Security to support us when we reach age 60. Yet, if we understood that we have the ability to double our substance, we would save $2,000 per year at a high yield. By age 60, we would have acquired enough substance to sustain ourselves exclusive of Social Security.

Often, we transfer our ignorance of adequate financial preparation to our children---we fail to think generationally. Because of this perennial lack of knowledge, each generation has to start afresh in learning how to prosper. For example: if your great grandmother had invested $1.00 at 12 % interest, the compound would have earned $32 within a year. That dollar would have earned her $1,024.00 in 60 years. In 90 years, that same dollar would have earned $32,768.00!

Prophetic Principle #5

Investing time is more valuable than investing money.

Can you imagine how you would feel if your parents presented you a check for $32,768.00 and told you that your great-grandparents invested $1.00 for you 90 years ago? This shows you the significant impact that you could have upon your future generations if you learn to apply time and interest!!

What if an individual invested $10,000 at a rate of 12 percent over a period of 12 years? They would acquire $40,000. Over a period of 24 years, they would have earned $160,000. In 36 years, they would have $640,000. In 48 years, they would have approximately 2.5 million dollars!!

Does this excite you? Does it motivate you? Well, here's one more example: If you were to invest $10,000 at 18 percent interest for 12 years, you'd accumulate $80,000, for 24 years, you'd have $640,000, and in 36 years, you'd have $5,120,000.00! and in 48 years, you'd have saved up a whopping $40,000,000 dollars!!

When Jesus talked about the stewards who had doubled their money, I began to ask, "How can I double my money?" I critically analyzed some of the world's systems. Some of us could have been much further along financially if we would have sacrificed by setting some money aside instead of succumbing to our fleshly demands for instant gratification. The money we have wasted foolishly would have been working to double our increase.

Statistics show that more than 75 percent of Americans could not survive if their homes experienced extensive damage due to a fire or storm.

They would be thrust into a state of financial ruin...they'd become homeless. That is a sad statistic. Therefore, we need to keep a portion of everything that we earn to invest in our future. I am not referring to investing your money one week, then getting it back around Christmas time to buy gifts. That is not a long-term addition to your substance. It simply makes it easier for you to spend and gratify your desires.

In my opinion, teller machines are money traps, therefore, I do not use them. They offer you easy access to your money and are designed to make it easy for you to continually withdraw your substance. The deception is that you will never allow your money to grow. If you want to walk in prosperity, it is critical for you to discipline yourself to save a part of your earnings for the purpose of increase and growth, so that your money will start to work for you.

Prophetic Principle #6

Prosperity requires discipline.

Because of the yoke of indebtedness, many people never experience life's enjoyment. After they've attended college for 4 or 8 years, they have to spend the next 8 to 15 years working to repay their student loans. They also become disillusioned because they do not secure a job in their planned area of expertise.

It becomes difficult for your children to enter the real estate market because of our economy's increased financial demands upon them. However, if finances had been saved in preparation for their future, then their generation would have excelled yours. If you were to put away finances for your son for the exclusive purpose of a home purchase, then he would not have to struggle to obtain property for his family in years to come.

Again, time is an important element concerning money. It is applicable even when you are buying a house. I believe that a 30 year mortgage is a trap to keep you in financial bondage to the bank. Within the 30 years of that mortgage, you will have paid for that house three times!! The first six or seven years of payments only goes towards the interest on the mortgage. It is amazing that if you have the foresight to obtain a 15 year mortgage instead, you can pay off the same property without doubling your cost. You may end up paying just $200 more each month, depending on the price of the property.

We must begin to use our financial resources wisely and strategize for increase. It is God's will for us to have money. He does not desire us to work all of our lives serving money, but He wants our money to work for us so that we can obtain wealth. Don't be like the unwise servant who buried his substance and cut off his avenue for financial gain. It is now time to seek the Father's face to allow Him to give us the strategy for creating an outlet for our money to flow.

Chapter Two
Creating An Outlet
Utilizing the Borrowed Substance

"Now there cried a certain woman of the wives of the sons of the prophets unto Elisha, saying, Thy servant my husband is dead; and thou knowest that thy servant did fear the Lord: and the creditor is come to take unto him my two sons to be bondmen.

And Elisha said unto her, What shall I do for thee? tell me, what hast thou in the house? And she said, Thine handmaid hath not anything in the house, save a pot of oil.

Then he said, Go, borrow thee vessels abroad of all thy neighbours, even empty vessels; borrow not a few.

And when thou art come in, thou shalt shut the

door upon thee and upon thy sons, and shalt pour out into all those vessels, and thou shalt set aside that which is full.

So she went from him, and shut the door upon her and upon her sons, who brought the vessels to her; and she poured out.

And it came to pass, when the vessels were full, that she said unto her son, Bring me yet a vessel. And he said unto her, There is not a vessel more. And the oil stayed.

Then she came and told the man of God. And he said, Go, sell the oil, and pay thy debt, and live thou and thy children of the rest."

2 Kings 4:1-7

The Bible says that the borrower is "servant" to the lender. If we can understand the purpose of borrowing, we will discern why and when we should borrow. Borrowing is only good when it is profitable.

When you borrowed in Biblical times and did not repay, penalties such as liens being placed on your property did not exist. However, when you borrowed in those days and did not repay, you were the personal guarantee.....they would enslave you. It was as if you signed the contract in blood.

The widow woman identified in II Kings, chapter four, was in a dilemma. The Scripture indicates that *"the curse causeless does not come"*. The story opens up

16

Prophetic Principle #7

Borrowing is only good when it is profitable.

with the widow's sons nearing enslavement because of an outstanding debt.

In verse three, Elisha instructed the widow to: *"Go, borrow thee vessels abroad of all thy neighbours, even empty vessels; borrow not a few."* I thought it was interesting that the prophet told the widow to "go borrow".

The widow's creditors wanted to take her two sons into bondage. They would have been slaves until the debt was paid in full. If some of you were living in those days, you would still be working to pay off your debt!

It is not wrong to borrow if you can borrow to generate more income. Also, borrowing is not evil as long as you can repay what you borrow at any time. If you desire to borrow $10,000 and you cannot determine how it would generate you $20,000, then you probably need not borrow. You cannot afford to borrow to that degree. On the other hand, if you borrow to invest in a car dealership, where you can anticipate generating a profit worthy of the loan, that is good. If you borrow to enjoy a vacation, that is foolish. All borrowing causes increased indebtedness, then it is evil.

You end up borrowing at 12 or 13 percent interest that will eventually choke the flow out of your finances and hold you captive. Besides, when you are in debt you are under extreme stress. It is very difficult to stay focused when you cannot pay your bills. Debt is a terrible thing......it is a monster.

One person explained the principle of borrowing by saying, "Borrowing is stripping your future to enhance your present." You need to seek a God-given idea, an avenue or a channel that will create more substance.

The prophet not only instructed the widow to borrow some vessels, but he told her to borrow empty vessels. That allowed her to create a vacuum. If there is no vacuum, then you are inhibiting God from continuing the supply. The prophet said, "Sell the oil and go pay off your debt." This confirms that borrowing should only be used for the purpose of creating more substance. You borrow to generate and then you pay off your debt.

Prophetic Principle #8

If borrowing causes increased indebtedness, then it is evil.

If you are in debt today, your answer is not in obtaining a consolidation loan. It is nice that you only have one creditor knocking on your door instead of five, however, you still have not answered the problem. You only brought about a temporary panacea to a permanent situation. Debt reduction as a result of cutting back your spending is not a viable solution, either.

Our God is El Shaddai. He is the God that teacheth us to profit. He gives us the power to get wealth. We should not seek debt resolution by reducing spending, but find more innovative ways to create more substance. I tell individuals that they do not have a money problem, but an idea problem. You have to create an outlet for God to add more increase to your life.

Prophetic Principle #9

"Borrowing is stripping your future to enhance your present.".

I believe that when you give financial seed, it can create a vacuum for God to provide the increased substance. The widow woman took the borrowed vessels for the purpose of increasing her substance. Then she was able to pay her debt in full.

Many businesses would not be in existence today if they did not have the opportunity to borrow. However, the principle is that you never set out to borrow at the point when you need financial resources. By this I mean that usually when you need a $20,000 loan within a week's time frame, you will not get an approval if it is your first time applying.

Prophetic Principle #10

God teaches us to profit.

Establishing a line of credit is a better idea for obtaining money when you need it. You can also have your account arranged so that funds would be available to you if an investment at an excellent rate was made available. Then, you can always put your hands on the extra finances instead of being under the stress or strain of trying to borrow at the last moment.

Using What is in Your Hands

"And Elisha said unto her, What shall I do for thee? tell me, what hast thou in the house? And she said, Thine handmaid hath not anything in the house, save a pot of oil."

II Kings 4:2

I believe that the Lord is asking us, *"What do you have in your hands?"* When we beseech Him in the midst of our dilemmas, He asks us, "What is within your reach?"

All too frequently, we do not use what is in our hands. We do not use the talent that the Father has given us. Talent is the key to greatness! There are tools of greatness lurking on the inside of you.

Acres of Diamonds was a book that talked about a man in Africa who sold his house to go and search for diamonds. He traveled all over the world seeking diamonds, and finally, at the end of his journey, he fell into a fit of despair because he did not realize his goal. In his pain and frustration, he jumped into the ocean and killed himself.

Prophetic Principle #11

Talent is the key to greatness!

Another man went to the house that the deceased gentleman had sold in his search for diamonds. He looked at a rock in the back yard that caught his trained eyes, and put it through a test. He said, "Oh, the man finally found his rock."

The man who unsuccessfully searched the world for diamonds had diamonds right in his back yard! He couldn't recognize them! The moral of the story is that you often look everywhere else for success except in your own back yard. You travel all over the world looking for an opportunity, or a future, and yet on the inside of you there are acres of diamonds and wealth untold that you fail to discern. You should stop looking outside of yourself for your treasure, because God placed it in an earthen vessel.

The Mentality of "Only"

The prophet said to the widow, *"What do you have in your house?"*

She replied, *"Thine handmaid hath not anything in the house, save a pot of oil."*

Prophetic Principle #12

Rid your vocabulary of the word "only."

The thing that appears insignificant in the face of your dilemma is the outlet that God wants to operate through to create wealth and bring you into greatness.

Usually, a person who is in poverty will connect the concept of **"only"** with the substance that God has given him. You must rid your vocabulary of the word **"only."** When you say the word **"only,"** then you are focusing on your lack instead of the substance and potential that God has given you.

When you say, **"I only"** have one thousand dollars, you are focusing on the thousands that you do not have. When you say, **"I only"** have ten dresses, you are focusing on all the other dresses that you do not have. If you say, **"I only"** have two cars, then you are focusing on all the other cars that you do not have.

The widow said she did not have anything in her house, save a pot of oil. She had a mentality of lack. She had a mentality of **"only."** She was unable to perceive an increase in her substance. This is why the devil magnifies what you do not have to make you feel insignificant in the face of your situation.

Prophetic Principle #13

A God-given idea is sitting in you.

Instead of you lifting up your hands and thanking God for what He has blessed you with, satan influences you and causes you to concentrate on what you do not have. You should be blessing God for the substance that He has put in your possession!

Many of you have said, "I don't have anything but a high school diploma and the ability to bake." Baking made Famous Amos famous! Cooking made Colonel Sanders rich! While you are focusing on your **"only,"** God is saying, "I want to get in your **"only"** and bring you into greatness, for you have potential that I can use, expand, and move through." God so loved that He gave His **"only"** begotten Son, and look at the fruit that came forth through Him!!

The prophet wanted to know what was in the widow's possession so that the power of God could MOVE!! God wants to work through what is already in YOUR possession! All too often, we look outside of ourselves. God says, look within.

Prophetic Principle #14

Voluntary giving is God's plan for increase.

One man told a story that contains a principle that we need to learn. The story goes like this:

When man fell, God said, "Where will I hide his divinity?" An angel said, "Let's put it in space", but God said, "No, because man will build rockets and go out into space and find it." Another angel said, "Let's put it in the depths of the sea," but God decided, "No, man will build submarines and go down in the depths of the sea and find it."

As the question was pondered by all the heavenly host, God said, "I know....we will put the spark of divinity right within man because this way, he will have to look within himself to find it."

Usually we are looking all outside of ourselves for help when God has spoken unto us and said, "You have a treasure in your earthen vessel." You have potential on the inside of you that has not even been developed, but it is waiting to escape, to come forth, and leap forward from obscurity so that it can begin to work for you and bring you to a new level of prosperity.

Prophetic Principle #15

Miracles are produced through the act of obedience.

A God-given idea is sitting in you. All you have to do is get up and start doing, instead of sitting and waiting. Stop waiting for your ship to come in, get in the boat and row to where the ship is!

Keys to Creating a Vacuum

1. Use what you have as a point of reference.
2. "Only" denotes that you are focusing on your lack.

3. Identify what you have with God's unlimited substance.

4. Become aware of the Omnipresence of God.

Practice His Presence. Say, *"Lord, I know that you can get in anything that I have in my possession. If it is an ability to sing, You are going to tell me what to do with my voice. If it is an ability to write, You will instruct me and tell me what to do with that ability."* Whatever you have, God wants to get in it so that He can cause it to multiply.

Stop putting God in a box by telling Him which way you desire His blessing to flow. God may have you go a way that may be unorthodox in order to get the prize. He won't cause you to go a way of compromise, but you must stop squeezing God in a box as to how things should happen.

Prophetic Principle #16

We must learn the laws of acquisition.

Some of you, if the prophet came to you and told you to borrow empty vessels you would say, "Wait a minute, me? My pride is in the way." If you are going to experience the increase of God, your pride has to be moved out of the way.

5. **Stop being part of the problem and become part of the solution.**

6. **God desires to manifest His Kingdom through you.**

The more necessary any element is to the sustaining of life, the more abundance of it will be available. There is an abundance of air, water, shelter, and food. In other words, God would never create a planet where there were not enough resources to sustain His creation. That's why we must learn that our financial troubles are never due to a money shortage, but rather, that we have not learned the laws of acquisition.

When men begin to absorb the lie that they don't have to work, or refuse to work, they become beggars who expect to receive support without contributing. Voluntary giving is God's plan for an individual's development. If you are going to develop or increase, you are going to have to give. The Bible says *if you give, it shall be given unto you, good measure, pressed down, shaken together, and running over shall MEN give into your bosom* (Luke 6:38).

Prophetic Principle #17

Failure is only a temporary setback.

The prophet asked the widow what she had in the house. She responded, **"Only a pot of oil."** A miracle was about to take place. The miraculous is connected with the act of obedience. If she would have never borrowed the vessels, she would have never had the substance.

Miracles are produced through the act of obedience. Your miracle is waiting on you to become obedient.

Again, opportunity does not waste its time with the unprepared. Opportunity surrounds you everyday, but it only spends time with those who are prepared to seize the moment.

Substance will only increase as long as there is a vacuum for it to expand into. Some of you want the increase to continue, but God says, "You haven't made a vacuum."

Sometimes you have to get rid of what is in you so that you can draw what should come to you. You will only draw to you what is already in you. For instance, if you connect with people who lack productivity, then you won't lead a productive life. You have to find the people with which God desires you to associate.

Prophetic Principle #18

The moment a task has been assigned to you, the devil assigns your opposition.

Even in the animal kingdom, each species finds its connection. At a farm, the chickens hang together and the pigs hang together. They walk in groups. The birds find their connection; they are not mixed up with all different types of species. You have to find those with whom you are ordained to fly. I like looking for those who fly high like eagles....who know how to fly beyond the realm of the clouds.

Some of us haven't tasted the sweetness of victory because we have not gotten rid of what is in us. For instance, look at the pig. You can take it out of the pigpen, clean it up, put a pretty bow around it, perfume it, and keep it in an environment which is nice, neat, clean, and sweet. After awhile, a pig can only stay in that environment so long and then its true nature will begin to surface. As soon as that pig gets a break for some mud, it knows where to go because that is his home. You will not change what you attract until you first change what is in you.

You will not see victory in God or become prosperous until you get rid of a poverty mentality. You are like a magnet; a force that pulls things to you. That is why prosperity must begin from the inside.

Joseph is an example of an individual who used what God had given him. He was down in the dumps due to his negative experiences. He was sold into slavery and was unjustly sent to prison. He could have said, "I did not deserve this," and consequently become bitter towards God.

What you may perceive as a failure is only a temporary setback. This is obvious in Joseph's case. God allowed Joseph to use his gift while he was in prison and it brought him to greatness. The Bible says in Proverbs, Chapter 18:16, that a man's gift will make room for him. God has already made room in the earth for the gift or talent that He has given you!

You should really thank God for the gift that He has given you! Whatever gift that God has given you it should not produce pain, but joy. If a person has a gift to play the piano, they must appreciate it in order to become proficient. He doesn't sit down at the piano and say, "God is making me do this. I can't take it anymore! Aah!." If God gifted you with computer expertise, you are not going to sit at the computer crying, "I wish that I could do something else."

The talent that is going to bring you to greatness will first produce joy in your life. You will love operating in your gift. If a person is going to be a skillful artist, he will not say, "God has given me this gift that I have to utilize." He does not say, "It hurts me when I have to pick up the pen to draw." When a person knows that being an artist is his purpose, he will embrace it. Even if he experienced a tragedy, and lost his hands, he would learn how to draw with his feet. He would not look for another skill to fit his situation. He will say, "This is what I am and I am going to fulfill my purpose."

Four Keys to Your Financial Success

1. **Problems must always be seen as opportunities for growth.**

Every problem that comes into your life must be seen as an opportunity for growth. Problems are not ordained for you to run from them, but they are ordained for your growth.

2. **Images (self-images and your thought life) that are left unchecked will take root in your life. No one can make you feel insecure without your permission.**

The prophet had to change what was in the widow's mind before he could change what was in her hands. He told her to go borrow vessels so that she could create an outlet for the increased substance. He could not leave her with that statement, but he had to deal with her mind. He said, "Don't borrow a few, go borrow plenty." She would have probably gone out with a small mentality and only borrowed one vessel. She would not have had enough to create the substance.

Prophetic Principle #19

You should refuse to be normal.

3. **People can't make you feel inferior without your consent.**

4. **A man isn't great because he hasn't failed, but because failure was not able to stop him.**

God never promised that you were not going to come forth without a struggle. The moment a task has been assigned to you, the devil assigns your opposition. With every new step of faith in life, there are enemies that are assigned to you. With every new door, there is new opposition. With every new level, there is a higher power of opposition.

Don't think that everyone will be happy if you succeed. Some people are happy if you fail because it eases the conviction on the inside of them. If you make it, it will convict them. Misery loves company.

People take pleasure in your being average. They think, "Well, you're average...just don't dare go above average." You must fight that enemy called "Average," "Mr. Mediocrity", "Mrs. Staying at the Norm". You should refuse to be normal!

Usually the people who became great inventors were the individuals who were called "crazy" or "off". The Wright brothers were examples of greatness. Thomas Edison is another example; he set out to make candles, which was a daily tool of life, into a luxury of the rich.

Things are changing, you cannot be normal! When someone tells you that you are doing average, don't get happy, but BE ANGRY!!

Chapter Three
Receiving the Word of the Lord

In II Kings, Chapter four, the widow identified her need to the Prophet. The Prophet is the carrier of the Word of the Lord. If he cannot get the Word out of you, the enemy will try to remove you from the connection...from the place where the Word dwells. Once he finds that the Word of the Lord is not in you, he will attempt to disconnect you from people who do have the Word of the Lord in them.

The devil will always try to remove you from the individual that the Word of the Lord is in or the place where the Word of the Lord is going forth. That is why the enemy attempts to deceive people into not attending church service. He knows that if you are at the place where the Word of the Lord is, then you are just one step away from receiving your miracle; your answer; your deliverance out of a dilemma, or your divine link. If the widow would have never made it to the prophet, she would never had made it to her place of divine provision.

If you are in a place where there is no Word flowing, you will be in famine. The widow woman's barrel did not increase until the Word made it into her home. The fish and the loaves did not multiply until the Word made contact with the little boy.

The water did not turn into wine until the Word spoke. The fish did not jump into the net until the Word said, "Let down thy net." In spite of what your circumstances look like, when the Word speaks and the Word of the Lord comes, no matter WHAT is in the way, the Word will come to pass!!

> *"Surely the Lord God will do nothing but He revealeth his secret unto his servants the prophets."*

Amos 3:7

Prophetic Principle #20

If you are in a place where there is no Word flowing, you will be in famine.

The widow knew where to find the man of God. She knew that the Prophet was the key to the miracle. Before God does anything in the earth, He will first reveal it through a Prophet. Before God does anything in your life, He will first send a special revelation. That is why I love when the Word of the Lord is released, for that means miracles are about to happen!

Prophetic Principle #21

Often, your miracle is in a place where you do not want to go!

Naaman, the Captain of the host of the king of Syria, had leprosy, but the handmaiden had to take the leper to the Word of the Lord. The Word of the Lord was in the prophet's mouth.

When the Word of the Lord comes, it may not be to your liking. To Naaman it was, "Go jump in the lake." Naaman's response was, "Wait a minute, do you know who I am?"

I have found that the Holy Ghost will have you do what you do not desire to do; He will confront you with the things that you said, "I will never do..." People with whom you do not want to have any dealings with, those are the ones with whom God commands you to connect.

It would do you good not to have a problem with a certain ethnic group because those are the type of people whom God will send right in your midst. You may try to go in another direction, but you will end up falling on your face. You will eventually have to connect and work with those very same individuals.

Prophetic Principle #22

Success is measured by how willing you are to take risks.

Don't tell God where you won't go or what you won't do because He has some news for you! Again, to Naaman, He said, "Go jump in the Jordan River" for that was the place of his assignment. That was the place of his miracle. Often, your miracle is in a place where you do not want to go!

Risks - Critical to Success

Success is measured by how willing you are to take risks. If you were afraid to take risks, you would not even go to an interview for fear of your application being denied. You would not write a speech for fear of no one being there to hear you. You might not go to work one day because you may lack the type of response that you desire. Risk-taking is imperative to success.

Nothing is 100 percent guaranteed. In other words, you are going to have to take risks. Those who are the most successful have taken the most risks. Those who acquire fruit have to go out on the limb. Those who are on the cutting edge, live on the edge!

Statistics show that of all millionaires, usually 37% end up losing all of their investment, yet they recover. They understand that money and ideas are just tools. They see many more tools to utilize as vehicles to obtaining wealth.

There is a power shift going on in the economy and the shift is currently causing it to rise and fall. The ones who are in trouble are the ones who are unwilling to change; the ones who are trying to play the 90's economic game with the 80's and 70's rules. While these are the worst days for some, these are going to be the best days for others because they will understand that the rules of the game are changing. They will be risk takers.

Prophetic Principle #23

Risk-taking is imperative to success.

There are God-given ideas that are sitting on the inside of you. God is waiting for you to birth them because He is not going to do it for you.

You are just one step away from your miracle! You are just one step away from a divine connection or link. All you have to do is connect with the purpose of God and you will find yourself on the road to victory.

God Honors His Word

When you give to God what belongs to Him, you will find that He honors His Word. The law of cause and effect says that, "For every act you will reap a reaction". For every seed or every deed, you will reap a harvest. Everything that you sow, you will reap.

The principle of seed time and harvest says that your seed is going to produce a harvest. You have to determine whether you are really willing to eat from the harvest of the seed that you are about to sow. Sometimes you want to sow the seed, but you do not want the weight of the harvest. There should always be excitement connected with the sowing of the seed.

Prophetic Principle #24

Money and ideas are just tools.

The same principle is true when it comes to sowing into another man's ministry. Whatever you make happen for a man of God, God makes sure that He makes the same thing happen for you.

One man of God was watching a particular preacher on television and he began making fun of him as he pleaded for a certain amount of money in order to continue in television ministry. He responded, "I don't believe that." Then, he said, suddenly, the Holy Spirit convicted him. The man didn't voice his sarcasm out loud, but he had only spoken in his heart, "He is just asking for money, it is just another gimmick."

Prophetic Principle #25

"For every act you will reap a reaction."

At the moment of that conviction, God told that man of God to send the television evangelist an offering. That was the only way he could be released from that conviction. God made him sow a seed. That is a principle. However you treat a man of God in adversity, that will be the same way that God will treat you when you experience your calamity.

Another man of God was viewing a preacher on television. The preacher was saying *"We have serious needs here..."*

He responded, *"So, do I."*

The preacher continued *"...And if you do not give, we are going off the air."*

The man responded, *"Well, nobody told you to go on the air anyway."*

The preacher said, ***"If you don't give, we are going to have to cut back on our stations."***

He said, *"Well, just get on off the air."*

Immediately, the Holy Spirit convicted him and said, ***"Sow a seed."***

I watch individuals who say, "I don't like that preacher, 'cause all he does is ask for money." I don't believe anything he says." Those will be the individuals for whom God will say, "Support them." That will be the key to their miracle. I have found that the reason something irritates you may be because God has called you to be raised up to solve the problem.

Prophetic Principle #26

**You are only one relationship away
from the palace.**

As you unlock the dreams of others in the season of your affliction, God is sovereignly raising up others who will unlock your dreams. The only way your dream is going to be unlocked is for you to unlock someone else's dream. You are only one relationship away from the palace and you must unlock the dream of those who hold the key to the fulfillment of your dreams.

Usually God's blessings come in disguised packages. It may have been a mate that God was sending in your direction. Nevertheless, you were so busy examining the package that you failed to search the substance. Ten years down the road you'll say, "I missed it. I know I should have married that one; that was a good catch." You were too busy looking at the package, so you missed the substance.

Prophetic Principle #27

Usually God's blessings come in disguised packages.

Oftentimes, God sends your blessing through the raven; through a package that you don't like very much. God will raise up individuals with whom you have the greatest amount of problems with to be the key or the connection in your life. It may be a Peter who had a problem with the Gentiles or a Paul who had problems with the Church. God will always raise up individuals with whom you have a problem and say, **"That is your divine connection."**

The individuals with whom you have problems are the same individuals that God will send your deliverance through. That is why there are some places that I have to go because there are some people who have problems with me. They hold the key to some of my victories.

If you keep the covenant of God concerning giving, then even when times are hard you will say, "I don't even know how I am making it." I don't even know how the bills are getting paid, but they are getting paid. I do not know how the money is coming in, but when the need must be met, it is met. Your faith in God's financial system is providing the substance for you in your time of need.

Prophetic Principle #28

Receiving the Word of the Lord through an anointed vessel is key to your miracle!

God always honors His Word. The Word of God will not return unto Him void. It will always accomplish that which it was sent to bring forth. God has established men and women who are ordained to carry His Word. That is why you must be open to receive from anointed vessels of God. Receiving the Word of the Lord through an anointed vessel is key to your miracle!

Chapter Four
The Firstfruit: The Key to Your Financial Breakthrough

"And in the process of time (the literal translation means, "at the end of days") it came to pass, that Cain brought of the fruit of the ground an offering unto the Lord.

And Abel, he also brought of the firstlings of his flock and of the fat thereof. And the Lord had respect unto Abel and to his offering."

Genesis 4:3-4

This scripture reveals that tithing and offering did not begin under Israel, but it began with Cain and Abel. We need to understand the seriousness of offering. It sends a signal to God.

Our offering tells God what we think about the Kingdom and how He is handling business. It lets Him know whether we are trusting in His Kingdom or the kingdom of the world.

God requires our firstfruit. The Apostle Paul said we are to lay up for the first day of the week what we are to bring unto God. We are to honor the Lord with the firstfruits of all of our increase.

Prophetic Principle #29

God requires our firstfruit.

When Cain and Abel's offering went up to God, the smoke from the offering had to ascend a certain way. The Lord observed it as it came before Him. This is why it is recorded that when Nadab and Abihu offered a strange fire, they were destroyed. The smoke from the offering went up before the Lord and was unacceptable. That indicates that God does not accept every offering.

In Israel, one could not offer just any type of calf or lamb unto the Lord. He required a tenth. If one decided to keep the tenth and just give Him the eleventh, then He would say, "Give me the tenth and the eleventh." In other words, if God speaks to you and says, "Sow ten dollars" and you sow five instead, you would have to sow 15 dollars to compensate for your disobedience. Disobedience always costs you!

We must understand the purpose of God, the mind of God, and His principles. When we hear the Father speak, we must learn how to respond because the speaking of the Lord is the key to our deliverance. God knows what is in store for our tomorrow. He knows what action we need to take today in order to produce the necessary reaction for tomorrow. He knows the struggle we must endure today in order to have victory tomorrow.

Are You Tipping God or Tithing?

"And in the process of time it came to pass, that Cain brought of the fruit of the ground an offering unto the Lord."

Genesis 4:3

Abel brought the **"firstling"** and the fat thereof. Abel brought the portion that was ordained for God, it was as if he was tithing. Cain did not bring the first fruit, instead, he brought an offering.

Prophetic Principle #30

If your tithe is not released, you have not given God an offering.

45

Many people in the Body of Christ are only tipping God, but they are not tithing. Abel's acceptance had nothing to do with him bringing a blood sacrifice, but God was pleased with the "firstling." God wants the tithe. Abel not only brought the firstling, but he also brought the fat thereof. Cain only brought an offering, but it really wasn't an offering because it wasn't acceptable to God.

Prophetic Principle #31

Whatever position you are in right now is a direct result of the dime.

Your offering really doesn't become a true offering until you first release the tithe. If your tithe is not released, you have not given God an offering. God doesn't even consider it an offering, nor a seed. He yells down from the heavens and says, "Unacceptable!!"

Some may say that tithing is an Old Testament principle because the New Testament only makes reference to offering. It is assumed that you know the tithe belongs to God. Tithing was the minimum requirement as it relates to giving!

I visited a church once where they believed in the "New Covenant". They said, "We were released from the law. We don't preach tithing here. We just tell people to bring a willing offering." I said, "That's nice, but God wants the bare minimum which is the tenth of all your increase." The tithe is His tax. That is our tax for living in the earth.

Whatever position you are in right now is a direct result of the dime. God requires a dime out of every dollar. If you are blessed, it means you have given Him the dime. If you are cursed, that means you held on to God's dime.

Giving By Faith

Now faith is the substance of things hoped for, the evidence of things not seen.

Hebrews 11:1

Faith has the ability to take that which is invisible and make it visible. It has the ability to take that which is in your future and bring it into your present. It will cause you to understand that you do not see with your natural eyes, but that you see with your mind. Your natural eyes can deceive you, only your renewed mind reveals to you the truth.

Prophetic Principle #32

Thoughts are "things."

When you view the ocean from the shore, it seems as though the water and the sky meet. Yet we know that is not true. When you are in a plane, it looks as if everything on earth is as small as ants. Your eyes lie to you.

The children of Israel said Goliath was too big to hit, but David said, "He is too big to miss". They saw themselves as grasshoppers. How you perceive yourself will determine how others perceive you. This is why it is critical for your mind to be renewed by the Word of God.

Prophetic Principle #33

The opposite of faith is fear.

When the Prophet told the widow woman to go borrow pots, she could have taken a philosophical stance and said, "Listen, I have my pride and I do not borrow my neighbor's pots. If you can't get vessels from my house, then we will not have any vessels around here." The oil would not have multiplied in that situation.

Elisha instructed the widow to "Borrow not a few,"she was told to borrow as much as she had faith to believe. In essence, your destiny and future is in your hands.

Many of you are saying, "God, I don't know why this breakthrough is not happening. Why aren't things taking place for me?" You need to dream big!!

You may think that you need more faith, but the Bible says that to every man has been given the measure of faith. It is already in you!!

When you give your tithes and offering unto the Lord, you are exercising your faith. Faith gives substance to "things" hoped for, to "things" that are connected to your future. If there are no "things," then there can be no faith. Faith reaches into your future and pulls the "things" that were ordained for you into your present. When you sow seed, have "things" in mind that you are hoping for and your faith will add the substance.

Thoughts are "things." That is why you have to be careful of what you think about, because one day your thoughts are going to break into action. If you prepare for a rainy day, it will rain.

Prophetic Principle #34

When you do not give unto God the offering that is due Him, your countenance will be disturbed.

You may ask, "What happens if the bottom falls out?" Then we will create the umbrella. However, I will not keep a room full of umbrellas, because I do not expect it to rain. Your faith gives substance to the very "things" for which you are hoping.

The opposite of faith is fear. Fear is destructive. Fear is **"False Evidence Appearing Real."** Your fear is satan's faith. The same way that faith moves God, fear moves the devil. When you have fear existing in your life, it will give substance to "things," but it will not yield the return that you desire.

Giving a More Excellent Sacrifice

By faith, Abel offered unto God a better sacrifice than Cain. Good is not good enough if better is available. God wants you to rise up above the norm. Abel offered a better sacrifice. Even though Abel was dead, the testimony of his giving did not cease. God testified on his behalf.

God looks at your gift so that He can testify. Your gifts will continue speaking throughout eternity. Cain's offering did not have such a pleasant testimony because God had no esteem or honor for his offering. When you become a giver, those who are not giving will despise you.

Prophetic Principle #35

As we begin to operate in the principles of God or the law of God, we will begin to live in victory.

Verse 6 says, *"And the Lord said unto Cain, Why art*

thou wroth? and why is thy countenance fallen?"

God barely spoke unto men in those days, yet He asked Cain, "Why is your countenance rough? Why are you upset? Why do you have an attitude? Why is your face down?" When you do not give unto God the offering that is due Him, your countenance will be disturbed. You will be angry. It will become obvious that God is not honoring you.

Prophetic Principle #36

"There is a wild beast crouching at the door waiting for your moment of disobedience."

I believe that one thing that God is doing in the area of giving is pushing the Church towards excellence. God is always producing keys in us and giving us principles. As we begin to operate in the principles of God or the law of God, we will begin to live in victory. You do not have to settle for second best!

Repentance and Obedience, The Way to God's Blessings

"If thou doest well, shalt thou not be accepted? and if thou doest not well, sin lieth at the door. And unto thee shall be his desire, and thou shalt rule over him."

Genesis 4:7

51

If you repent and be obedient, won't you be accepted? God is saying, "If you want My blessings, just operate in My laws; operate in that which is My purpose".

The phrase, "sin lieth at the door," literally means that "there is a wild beast crouching at the door waiting for your moment of disobedience". I envisioned this wild beast. It waits at the door to see if you are going to release the tithe to God.

I understand why the Bible says, "He will rebuke the devourer for your sake". Everyday the devourer is sitting at your door. When you tithe, you are insured. When you do not tithe, God says, "You have tied My hands. I can't do anything. The beast is released. Sin lieth at the door."

Prophetic Principle #37

The enemy of your soul is watching to see if you are going to fulfill your pledge.

Notice that verse seven says, *"and unto thee shall be his desires."* You become the appetite of that beast that is waiting to devour. He can't touch you as long as your covenant is intact.

God doesn't want you to have any dealings with the beast. However, if you do well, God will give you authority over your enemy. Instead of him ruling over you, you will rule over him.

The Curse of Robbing God

"Will a man rob God? Yet ye have robbed me. But ye say, Wherein have we robbed thee? In tithes and offerings."

Malachi 3:8

God told me that many people are in financial bondage because of the unfulfilled vows (pledges) that they have made. The enemy of your soul is watching to see if you are going to fulfill your pledge. When you do not fulfill it, he is like an avenging angel that is released to wreck havoc in your life.

God takes tithing and offerings personal. He said "When you do not give tithes and offerings, you have robbed Me. Therefore, you are cursed with a curse".

An entire nation had robbed God. He said they were cursed with a curse. If a curse is released in your life, maybe you withheld finances that belonged to God. That which is food to God can be poison to men, because He requires us to bring all the tithes into the storehouse that there may be "meat" in His house.

I believe that the "meat" was not as much natural food, but the spiritual food or the meat of revelation. If you want to be in a place that is flowing in revelation knowledge, then you need to be in a place where the people are tithing.

There was darkness for four hundred years between the books of Malachi and Matthew because an entire nation had robbed God. There was silence, and no revelation. The heavens were shut up.

Have the heavens seemed as though they have been like brass to you? Does it seem as though God has been silent in your situation? Does it seem as though when you pray, your prayers are hitting the ceiling and coming back? Could the reason be that you have not tithed?

Prophetic Principle #38

That which is food to God can be poison to men.

When you do not give your tithes and offerings, the heavens will shut. When you give the tithe and offerings, the heavens will open.

> *"...And prove me now herewith, saith the Lord of hosts, if I will not open you the windows of heaven, and pour you out a blessing, that there shall not be room enough to receive it."*

Malachi 3:10

God is saying **"I want you to put Me to the test. Try Me. Examine Me."**

Once, I was ministering in Idaho, and God moved tremendously. God challenged the people to give supernaturally. The last night of the meeting, supernatural things were happening with the people and they went away upset because they did not have more to give. The church received more money in those three days than they had ever witnessed. The pastor said, "Did you notice how rich the anointing was in here, how powerful it was in here, and the freedom that began to take place in the people?"

I found that the prophetic utterance was operating at a level of accuracy that I had not witnessed before. I asked, "Lord is this a new dimension that I am moving in?" He said, "No, it is because the people have opened up their pockets. I have opened the heavens in response to their obedience."

Prophetic Principle #39

Something spiritual happens when there is a release that costs you something.

God said, oftentimes, you feel as though the ministry gift vessel has to usher in the anointing. However, if the faith of the people is not at the proper level, it will affect the anointing. Even Jesus, who was God manifested in the flesh, could not flow in His full anointing in Nazareth because of the way that they perceived Him, and because of their unbelief.

I must have prophesied over everyone who was in the building that night because of the rich anointing. I could hardly teach because of the prophetic anointing. The Lord said that the faith of the people pushed the heavens open. Malachi, Chapter 3, became open to me as a fresh revelation. Every one of the services that I now conduct, God is saying, "Prove Me and see how far open you can get the windows." "Put me to the test and see how much you can get the heavens to open up for you."

When the widow woman gave her last meal, the heavens opened and her barrel was filled. When the little boy gave his lunch, the heavens opened. God blessed and multiplied the bread and fish. Something spiritual happens when there is a release that costs you something.

God wants to get you to the place where you tell Him "Enough, enough, enough Lord, shut the heavens! I have no more room!" When is the last time that your prayer has been "Enough, Lord?"

God said He would rebuke the devourer for our sake. God wants to bring the Church to a place of obedience. He wants to bring us to the place where we have more than enough.

God is just. He allows us to bring unto Him an excellent sacrifice in our giving. We choose whether or not we will be obedient in our giving. The choice is ours as to whether we want to release to God the tithe and offering in order to receive our financial breakthrough.

Chapter Five
Bringing Your Gift to the Altar

"And Noah builded an altar unto the Lord; and took of every clean beast, and of every clean fowl, and offered burnt offerings on the altar.

And the Lord smelled a sweet savour; and the Lord said in his heart, I will not again curse the ground any more for man's sake; for the imagination of man's heart is evil from his youth; neither will I again smite any more every thing living, as I have done.

While the earth remaineth, seedtime and harvest, and cold and heat, and summer and winter, and day and night shall not cease."

Genesis 8:20-22.

God allowed a flood to come on the earth because of the evilness of men. Man did not move into the purposes of God according to what He had ordained. Therefore, man went through a period whereby he experienced God's judgement.

Noah fulfilled his purpose. His purpose was to build an ark to save mankind. If you attempt to judge whether Noah was someone who was successful or not, you must not consider numbers. Success is not determined by numbers. If that were the case, then after 120 years of preaching, only 8 people were saved under Noah's ministry. Noah would have probably been listed as a failure as a preacher or leader in today's time. Success is determined by obedience. As long as you are in the center of God's will you are successful.

Altar, a Place of Sacrifice

The eighth chapter of Genesis is the first place where "altar" is mentioned. The English term of altar means, "a high place." It was commonly a raised structure.

One particular commentary stated that the altar was not required before the flood because God's divine Presence was still being visited among men at the gate of Eden. God even placed cherubims at the gate to assure that man would no longer enter the garden.

When we do not eat from the tree of life, we in turn will eat from the tree of the knowledge of good and evil. Frequently, individuals will substitute knowledge for life. I do believe in investing in the mind. However, the only way in which the mind can be renewed is through the Word of God.

There were several trees set in the garden of Eden. It wasn't an apple tree that man partook of, but it was a tree of the knowledge of good and evil. You can eat from the tree of the knowledge of "good" and it not be God. We have to learn to discern the difference between good and God.

Prophetic Principle #40

Success is determined by obedience.

When we bring our gift unto the Lord, we are to bring it unto the altar. The altar denotes the Presence of God. There was a visible place at the entrance of the garden of Eden for men to turn their hearts and offering toward the abode or the abiding place of the Lord.

Noah built his altar "unto the Lord." This actually meant that he built his altar unto Jehovah. He built his altar unto the One who could provide salvation, healing, and deliverance.

When we worship Jehovah in our giving, it brings liberation. Some of the keys to your deliverance are locked up in the financial seeds that you sow.

When you come to the altar, you come to the place where the Father is receiving sacrifice. The altar is where the transaction is made.

A couple came to Peter, but they did not realize that they were coming to the Holy Ghost because He was at the altar receiving the offering, though they thought it was a man. They were not destroyed because of what they gave, but because of what they withheld.

Withholding a portion that belonged unto the Father cost Ananias and Saphira their lives. Whatever Father demands of you, you had better give it to Him. A lot of times we sing, "I surrender all," but in reality we don't. We say, "Lord, I give it all to you." However, when He asks for it, we say, "Well Lord, I planned on using it for another purpose."

We sing the song, "I'm yours Lord, everything I got, everything I am, everything I'm not, I am yours Lord, try me now and see..." He says, "Okay, give $500 today." We respond, "Wait a minute. Try me tomorrow."

The Father is trying you. He wants to see who is your Lord. If you want to see an individual's obsession, just observe where he spends the most of his time and look at his checkbook. You can identify what kingdom he is investing in by examining his checkbook.

We must understand the law of sowing and reaping. When you sow a seed, you will reap a harvest. Every seed is a seed that is to be sown. Every act of obedience is going to produce a miracle in your life. You may consider tithes and offering a great sacrifice, but obedience is better than sacrifice.

God loves talking about offerings. He devoted an entire book, Leviticus, to offerings. Since He loves offerings, we have to learn how to celebrate and rejoice in giving. When we learn this, we will experience God's blessings.

Prophetic Principle #41

Understand the law of sowing and reaping.

Noah built the altar unto Jehovah God. Jehovah means, "the Lord is salvation." When you understand Him as Jehovah Jireh, it means "the Lord will "see to it," He is the one who will provide". The prefix "pro" equals two and "vide" equals video. Provision literally means "that He will "see to it;" with every God-given vision, there will be that which will be "pro" the vision.

The Bible says "Seek ye first the Kingdom of God and His righteousness and all these things shall be added unto you." There are many people in the Church who seek the Person of Christ, but not the principles of Christ. On the other hand, the world seeks the principles of God, but not the Person of God.

A corporation such as IBM is successful because its employees operate more in the principles of the kingdom than do the saints of God. There are some things that God does not want you to tolerate. If something is not producing, He doesn't want you to hang on to it, but rather, He wants you to curse it and leave it alone. We are the only people on the planet who will hang on to things that are subtracting from our lives!

Father wants to bring us into a place where we are going to connect with that which is adding to us...with that which will help us to promote the Kingdom. However, if it is going to take us away from the principles of the Kingdom we have to eliminate it from our lives. Even when Jesus looked at a fig tree that did not bear fruit, He cursed the tree.

The Fragrance of Your Offering

"...And the Lord smelled the sweet savour."

Genesis 8:21

The Lord smelled the offering that Noah made unto Him. It was a sweet smell. It meant that it was an offering of obedience.

The Lord also smells the offering that we bring unto Him. Does your offering have a sweet smell or an offensive smell in the Father's nostrils?

There are many people who send up an offering unto the Lord. When all the tithers in the house of God are asked to stand, and if you are not tithing and you are standing among them, you are lying. You are just attempting to be numbered among the tithers. When your offering hits the Father's nostrils, it is offensive to Him. What kind of smell does your offering have?

The Lord uses His nose. He inhales the fragrance through His nostrils. Father can't wait until offering time, so that He can inhale the fragrance of your offering. A sweet smell satisfies Him.

When something smells good, you want to remain in that atmosphere. If you want God to remain in your situation, then bring unto Him an offering that will produce results.

When you give, it is not a time where you feel as though a robbery has occurred. Your future is in your hands in the form of a financial seed. It has been in your hands all the time.

There are some offerings that I believe make God sick on the stomach. The Bible tells us that He said, "I would that you were hot or cold, if you are lukewarm I will spew you out of my mouth." There are some things that make Him sick on the stomach.

After having received your increase, it is time to bring your tithe unto the Lord. He may have just blessed you with $500 and something pressing just happens to surface. However, that is the time for you to release unto God a portion of the substance that He has already placed in your hands. He says that He wants the tax, the tenth.

When you begin to present your offering, He is smelling it to see if it is going to be a sweet savor or if it is going to make Him nauseous. God is smelling your offering to see if it is an offering of obedience or disobedience. When you bring an offensive offering, Father does not remain in the midst. When the aroma begins to fill His nostrils, He doesn't want to dwell there. Are you entertaining Father's Presence or are you driving His Presence away?

When you bring an offering unto the Lord and He is pleased, He dwells there and rebukes the devourer for your sake. He sees to it that while He is there, the enemy does not come near you. However, when He smells an offensive offering, He leaves and the enemy appears. The enemy loves dwelling around things that stink, things of disobedience. He is the father of disobedience and lawlessness.

Chapter Six
Making Friends With Unrighteous Mammon

"And he said also unto his disciples, There was a certain rich man, which had a steward; and the same was accused unto him that he had wasted his goods.

And he called him, and said unto him, How is it that I hear this of thee? give an account of thy stewardship; for thou mayest be no longer steward.

Then the steward said within himself, What shall I do? for my lord taketh away from me the stewardship: I cannot dig; to beg I am ashamed.

I am resolved what to do, that, when I am put out of the stewardship, they may receive me into their houses.

So he called every one of his lord's debtors unto him, and said unto the firs, How much owest thou unto my lord?

And he said, An hundred measures of oil. And he said unto him, Take thy bill, and sit down quickly, and write fifty.

Then said he to another, And how much owest thou? And he said, An hundred measures of wheat, And he said unto him, Take thy bill, and write fourscore.

And the lord commended the unjust steward, because he had done wisely: for the children of this world are in their generation wiser than the children of light.

And I say unto you, Make to yourselves friends of the mammon of unrighteousness; that, when ye fail, they may receive you into everlasting habitations.

He that is faithful in that which is least is faithful also in much: and he that is unjust in the least is unjust also in much.

If therefore ye have not been faithful in the unrighteous mammon, who will commit to your trust the true riches?

And if ye have not been faithful in that which is another man's, who shall give you that which is your own?

No servant can serve two masters: for either he will hate the one, and love the other: or else he will hold to the one, and despise the other. Ye cannot serve God and mammon."

Luke 16:1-13

The Master came to take account of the goods. He found an unfaithful steward....one who was not acting wisely with that which was under his administration or government.

Prophetic Principle #42

Money is just a means of exchange.

If money is not your friend, then money will not work for you, but it will work against you and become your enemy. The devil has told the Church for years that it doesn't need money, therefore, it is sinful to have financial substance. He told us that money is the root of all evil. That is not true. The Bible says that the "love" of money is the root of all evil. When you do not have any money, you are limited in terms of the things that you can accomplish. Money is just a means of exchange.

Evidently, the unwise servant in this passage knew that he was in a dilemma, so he became a giver. In his dilemma, he used the power that was reserved for him and he started giving to others....he began reducing debt. The throes of your trials or dilemmas is not the signal to withhold your finances. You must learn that the secret to your breakthrough is in giving.

The Lord commended the unjust steward because he acted wisely. Jesus said the children of this world are in their generation wiser than children of light. He said this because the children of light do not know how to handle money. Money can be a witness as to whether you are wise or foolish. Your ability to accumulate wealth will determine whether you are ignorant or whether you are wise. It will be a testimony for or against you.

Prophetic Principle #43

Money can be a witness as to whether you are wise or foolish.

In this parable, Jesus describes a man who starts to eliminate debt. He sees that his days of work are coming to an end, yet the man began giving and making friends with wealth.

It is time for the Church to become wise. Verse nine says, "I say unto you, make to yourself friends of the mammon of unrighteousness." If we are going to carry the gospel and the message of the Kingdom, we need wealth. The enemy does not want us to accumulate wealth. He knows that the more economical we are, the more potential we have to gain control. Our effectiveness will increase. We can change the lives of many individuals, if we can handle wisely this tool that God has placed in the earth.

When the woman with the alabaster box got ready to pour the oil on Jesus' feet, the disciples became disturbed because the alabaster box was worth a year's wages. She poured an entire year of wages on Jesus' feet. In today's economy that would be equivalent to $20,000. When is the last time you gave a year of wages to your Lord and Savior? Jesus did not turn her away though people thought He should have.

The disciples came up with a good suggestion, just as they would have in today's society. If Jesus walked into the room and someone said, "Jesus is here, good Master, I have $30,000 that I brought in oil and ointment that I can pour it on your feet." Someone would arise and say, "What about the homeless in New York City? Couldn't you have used the money for the homeless? Let's call the news. I can't believe they poured thousands of dollars on His feet in oil and ointment when we have those who are homeless living in boxes right across the street."

Jesus would have answered them and said, "The poor you have with you always, but me you won't have always." People would have said, "You see, He is ego tripping." Some people are not ready for this type of gospel, but they may as well start making preparation. It's a new day!

The things that God is going to bring us into are going to change the world. Whenever God gets ready to interrupt a cycle in history and bring change to the planet, He raises up mad men to complete the assignment. He raises up an Edison who says, "I want to create light through a bulb;" or the Wright brothers who said, "We think we want to fly." Think of how ludicrous that sounded in their day!

Prophetic Principle #44

You must dare to interrupt the cycle of the present to move into the cycle of your future.

Martin Luther King said he had a dream that every white boy and every black boy would join hands together. There are those who said he had a touch of madness. A Malcolm X who said, "By any means necessary," had a touch of madness.

In spite of their philosophy, the principle is that they dared to interrupt a cycle. You must dare to interrupt the cycle of the present to move into the cycle of your future.

One day people will look up and say, "Wow! These things came to pass! They were not as crazy and 'off' as we thought they were!" If you are one step ahead of people, you are a leader. If you are two steps ahead, you become a martyr.

Money Reveals Your Character

If you cannot be faithful in your money, then how can God trust you with spiritual gifts? How can He trust you with the true riches of the Kingdom? In other words, money has a way of exposing your character, it reveals who you really are. Money does not decrease you, it increases you. Money does not corrupt you, but it magnifies what you already are. If money corrupts you, why hasn't the devil overdosed you with it?

If you give a dope addict ten dollars, he will buy dope. If you give him one thousand dollars, he will buy more dope. If you give him a million dollars, he will still buy dope. If you give a gambler ten, one thousand or a million dollars, he will continue gambling.

If you give a man or woman of God, someone who minds the Kingdom, ten dollars they will sow it so that they can grow it back in the Kingdom. They will do the same thing with one thousand or a million dollars.

Again, money enhances who you already are in regard to your character. You may think that someone came into a large sum of money and then

73

turned evil, but they were already evil in their heart. Initially you were only looking at the seed, until the full harvest broke forth.

I understand why some people did not come into wealth a long time ago. There were even some things that God had to first work on the inside of me before He allowed me to come into financial blessings. Not everyone can handle money or power.

Prophetic Principle #45

Money does not corrupt you, but it magnifies what you already are.

God is watching you daily. He is watching to see if you are faithful in that which is someone else's. Your faithfulness with that which is someone else's will determine whether you will come into your own.

No Man Can Serve Two Masters

Jesus, who was God manifested in the flesh, only talked about two masters. God was one. Mammon was the other. You can't serve God and mammon. He brought mammon seemingly on the same level as God.

Money is the world's god. The world gets upset when you begin to talk about money. They say, "All that preacher on television does is talk about money.

We go to church and all they do is talk about money."
Preachers are attempting to release you from the
world's god. They are teaching you how to become
friends with mammon, instead of becoming its
servant.

How many of you are tired of money telling you
what you can or cannot do? The price tag is the first
thing you reach for on the dress in the store. The first
thing you ask an individual, even before you check
the quality of an item is, "What is the price?" The first
question that you ask in any instance is "How much
does that cost?" Money is the last thing discussed by
those who conquer mammon.

Prophetic Principle #46

Money is the world's god.

I never pay the listed price of anything that I
purchase. The salesman quotes me one price and I
hear another price in my spirit. He says, "I can't do
that for you." I say, "Yes you can...you can do all
things." When you walk out of their store, you can go
somewhere else, but they can't. The product is just
sitting there. Therefore, you can exercise some power.

If we would learn the power of networking, we
would tell merchants, "We want to come in here and
do this..." When you say, "we," they understand

numbers. "We" represents the community. You can also say, "We" have been here and "we" understand that you have not really been serving our community. "We" have some concerns". Money is a language that the world understands.

The Lord advises us to make friends with unrighteous mammon. He wants to equip us for wealth. The Bible says that the wealth of the wicked is laid up for the just. Again, money is not evil, but to love it is evil. When we begin to tap into the financial resources in the earth, then we can become a source of power for the building of God's Kingdom.

Chapter Seven
What Type of Ground Are You Sowing In?

"The same day went Jesus out of the house, and sat by the sea side.

And great multitudes were gathered together unto him, so that he went into a ship, and sat; and the whole multitude stood on the shore.

And he spake many things unto them in parables, saying, Behold, a sower went forth to sow.

And when he sowed, some seeds fell by the way side, and the fowls came and devoured them up:

Some fell upon stony places, where thy had not much earth; and forthwith they sprung up, because they had no deepness of earth:

And when the sun was up, they were scorched; and because they had no root, they withered away.
And some fell among thorns; and the thorns sprung up, and choked them."

Matthew 13:1-7

Reaping What You Sow

You will pass through some experiences before you get some real breakthroughs. You will reap whatever you sow. Even after you are forgiven and Jesus comes into your life, you will still reap from some of the past acts that you sowed.

Paul spent much time in prison. Have you ever wondered why? This was even after he received Christ into his life. Remember when he was throwing the Christians in prison and beating them? Notice that when he got born-again, his day of reaping came even though he was forgiven. Whatever you have done in the past will be reaped in the future.

If you sow kindness, you will reap kindness. If you sow mercy, you will reap mercy. If you sow love, you will reap love. If you want friends, you must show yourself friendly.

If you do not, you will not reap friends in life. One person said, insanity is doing the same thing over and over, yet expecting different results.

The egg is barren in seedtime. When you plant seed, that is usually the time when nothing is growing on your ground. You have to learn how to discern the seasons of God.

If you do not learn how to discern God's seasons, you will miss God. You may be looking for a particular season to be one of reaping, when it is the season of sowing. If you miss your season of sowing, you will miss the blessings of God in your life during harvest time. Therefore, you have to learn how to celebrate giving because your seed is going to determine your future harvest.

Prophetic Principle #47

You have to learn how to discern the seasons of God.

It takes a seed in order to reap a harvest. You have to work to sow. After you have the seed and you do the deed, you are going to have to work at cleaning up the weeds. Get rid of the weeds. There will always be weeds that will try to destroy what God wants to bring forth. There will always be an enemy to your harvest.

Every seed desires to grow and to operate at its maximum potential. There is something wrong if you do not desire to grow and achieve. Even by nature, a seed, when it is in the right environment, comes forth in its full stature. It, too, desires to grow up and be successful. You must discover the environment that the Father has called you to be sown in and you will grow to your maximum potential.

Sowing in the Right Ground

Sometimes you may be sowing a seed in your giving, but you might be sowing in the wrong place. If you sow your tithe somewhere else, you do not have it in the proper soil. If you are giving your tithe to your next door neighbor because he had a fire, that is good but it is not God. It will still produce death.

Sowing in the wrong ground could justify why you are not reaping a harvest. You are not a giver until you give over and beyond your tithe. The Bible says for us to honor the Lord with the firstfruits of all of our increase. We are to bring all of the tithes and offerings into the "storehouse," that there may be meat in His house.

Matthew 13:3 says, *"Behold a sower went to sow."* God has ordained you to sow. If you sow seed, God will make sure it grows. Often we say, "Lord if you bless me with this, then I am going to do that." Notice that it never works because that is not the nature of God. A farmer does not say, "Lord, if you grow corn on my field, I will plant corn next year." "Lord if you put apples in my back yard, I will sow apples next year."

You have to go find a seed to sow. People often wonder why they have never received financial breakthroughs in God, it is because they refused to plant a seed. If you refuse to plant a seed, you will never receive the fruit of the harvest. God does not want you on welfare, but He wants you faring well.

Prophetic Principle #48

A seed that has no entrance in the ground cannot show any life.

You do not have to become subject to a system and wait on a bread line. If you want to change the situation that you are in, you must start sowing seed in the proper ground.

Seed Sown by the Wayside

"And when he sowed, some seeds fell by the way side, and the fowls came and devoured them up:"

Matthew 13:4

The wayside represents "a hard place". No matter how valuable the seed, it will only fall on the ground. It will not have the ability to penetrate the ground because of its hardness. The seed that was planted by the wayside was good seed, but again, it is the place where you plant the seed that is significant. A person can sow one hundred dollars along with many others, yet his harvest is much greater than theirs. He knew what to do with his seed.

The seed is always in danger of being lost until it is hidden in the ground and out of your hands. The fowls came and ate it because it wasn't in the ground.

The loss is usually not felt because you do not know the worth that was in your seed. You may say, "I just lost one hundred dollars," when you may have just lost a million dollars. The one hundred dollars could have been the key to your million.

When I receive finances that I deserve, I ask God to confirm whether it is a harvest or a seed. One way to discern whether you have a seed or a harvest is this: if it is not big enough to meet your need, then it is a seed; it is not your harvest.

A seed that has no entrance in the ground cannot show any life. There are some of you whom God has blessed with seed, but you never allowed it to be sown into the ground that He ordained.

Some people are presently in financial dilemmas where they are not having a breakthrough. If they were to be honest, they would admit that there was a time when the Lord dealt with their heart to sow some seed and they responded, "Lord, I don't know if I can do that right now. That is a high thing to sow." As a result of their disobedience, they do not have the harvest that they need today.

The seed determines your future. It is up to you as to whether or not you are concerned about your future. Many of us strip our future to enhance our present.

Seed Sown on Stony Ground

"Some fell upon stony places, where thy had not much earth; and forthwith they sprung up, because they had no deepness of earth:

And when the sun was up, they were scorched; and because they had no root, they withered away."

Matthew 13:5-6

Prophetic Principle #49

The seed determines your future.

It amazes me as to the number of people who will sow into the lottery. They have more faith in the lottery than in the Kingdom. A Pastor once surveyed his congregation as to how much money they had sown into the lottery that month. Out of that congregation, thousands of dollars were sown into the lottery. Imagine if they would have sown it into the Kingdom of God to contribute to the spreading of the gospel!

If the Preacher would have said, "We want to go on television around the world and we want to send your seed around the world, so come and plant in this harvest," the people would have gotten an attitude. They would have said that the preacher asks for too much money, yet none of them complained when their lottery ticket did not win.

People don't become discontent with the state when they lose in the lottery. They don't say that the state is asking for too much money. They don't believe that the lottery is a rip off. They do not accuse them of being crooks. How do you know how they select the numbers? They could be showing you anything on television!

There are people who have more trust in the kingdoms of this world, such as the lottery, than in the Kingdom of God. The Father guarantees you a return if you act in obedience.

The stony ground meant that it did not have much earth. They sowed their seed, but it was very shallow. It did not have much depth. Some people sow just enough seed to see the return. If you sow a seed in someone's life looking for favors in return, you will not receive God's blessings. You can't sow for favors. It is better for you to have God's favor than to look for man to favor you.

Many people are sowing and looking for favors in return. I would rather have God's favor than the favor of man. When God favors you, He touches hearts. When He touches hearts, you don't have to look to give God anything in return. The Bible says that he that giveth to the poor lendeth to the Lord. God pays His debts.

Keys to Remember:

1. When you become a giver in the Kingdom, you will receive a return. When seed is not planted deeply, it will quickly starve. You have to plant your seed deep in the ground where it is out of sight. In other words, you must give it and forget that it was sown. If your seed is not out of sight, you did not plant it deep enough.

2. You have to sow your seed deep enough for the roots to be nourished because the roots will determine the strength of the seed. When you give, if it is not planted deep enough, you will not receive the harvest that God has ordained for you.

Prophetic Principle #50

Discouragement will cause you to lose
lasting results.

3. A quick return is not an everlasting return. Money that is received quickly is money that

does not last. Illegal money is like water going through your hands. He that maketh haste to get rich shall not be innocent. Get rid of "get rich quick" schemes.

In the laws of nature, you can't get a tree to grow overnight after you have planted the seed. It takes time to grow. Some people are discouraged between the period of the seed and the harvest. Discouragement will cause you to lose lasting results.

4. The seed is scorched because there was no depth. Your seed was overcome by the outward circumstances because there was no depth. To some, there are things in your life that were overcome by the outward circumstances because there was no depth in you or your seed.

Seed Sown Among Thorns

"And some fell among thorns; and the thorns sprung up, and choked them."

Matthew 13:7

There are enemies to your seed, anointing, calling, purpose, and soul. The moment you were born-again and said "yes" to Jesus, the devil assigned a principality to you. The moment you said "yes" to your calling, the enemy assigned it a principality. That is why Paul sought the Lord thrice, "Lord deliver me from this affliction." The Lord said, "My grace is sufficient."

Paul's affliction was that a messenger from satan was sent to buffet him. When you are called of God, there are messengers that are sent to buffet you in order to remove you out of the purpose and place of God. That is why everyone who is sent your way is not God-sent. Some people are satan sent to subtract the anointing from your life instead of adding to the anointing.

You have to learn how to discern relationships, friends with whom you connect. Everyone who greets you and smiles at you is not assigned to add to your anointing.

When there are thorns, it means that the soil is preoccupied. When there are thorns in the ground it will choke the seed that God has ordained. Subsequently, if there were thorns available to choke the seed, that means that there was not enough depth for the seed to grow properly. However, a seed can still grow amongst the thorns. In verse seven, we see that the thorns were already growing there. The weeds were sprouting. That means that the thorns were an obstacle or problem that could be reversed into an opportunity.

If your seed is going to grow, the thorns must be removed. You have to pull up the thorns. You must replace the unclean with the clean. Sometimes in order for you to plant in the ground that you desire, you have to remove some of the garbage that is in your mind that will choke the seed that you are trying to sow.

Seed Sown on Good Ground

"But other fell into good ground, and brought forth fruit, some an hundredfold, some sixtyfold, some thirtyfold."

Matthew 13:8

Good ground is a ground that is well worked. When a farmer sows seed, he first works it and surveys the ground to make sure that the ground is able to receive seed.

Weeds are destroyed in the good ground so it can't choke the seed. If you are going to see your harvest come forth, you will have to destroy the weeds in order for the ground to become fertile.

I believe that God told Adam to till the ground because He knew that there would be enemies in that ground. Adam had to dress and keep the ground. God would not have told Adam to keep it if there were no intruders.

God never gives you anything that will not be challenging. Your marriage will be a challenge. There are a lot of people who love each other and get a divorce. Love is not what holds a marriage together, but commitment. Covenant is not based on love, but commitment.

Two people who are adults that have entered into manhood or womanhood should understand that when they divorce, the individuals who suffer are the children. There are some cases that are extreme where God gives you a way of escape. However, the reality is that we have to become committed to each other.

In our local churches, we must become committed to each other. People don't like the word "commitment". They don't mind dating, but they're not quite ready for marriage. Commitment means "dirty socks" have to be washed. It means that you will see another side of them that you may not want to witness.

Prophetic Principle #51

Growth demands change.

If the seed is to be fruitful, your seed must have liberty in the soil. You can't take the seed out of the soil. You must leave it in the soil. Some people try to go in the soil and manipulate the seed. If your seed is to bring a return, you must sow it and forget about it; stop digging up your seed to see what is happening in the soil.

The seed must have time to germinate. Germination is the beginning of growth. Growth demands change. Your seed has to germinate under suitable conditions.

That means that your seed can't be in your cabinet or your wallet. You have to get it out of your hands and into good ground.

Sowing By Faith

Sowing seed must be done on battleground and the reaping of a harvest will be on the fruitful ground. When a farmer sows, he sows in faith. He has no guarantee of the weather conditions, he is trusting God.

When you invest in the Kingdom of God and sow out of the act of obedience, God will guarantee you a miracle. He will confirm His word with the signs following. If a farmer were to sow seed based upon the appearance of the soil, he wouldn't sow because usually the land is barren at seedtime. It doesn't look like there is any future in the soil. It is conceivable that he could hold his seed and life could go on like nothing happened. However, you can't obtain success before work. One person said, "The only way that success comes before work is in the dictionary." You have to work in order to reap success.

A farmer sowing seed compares to when you miss tithing for about a month or two. Let's say that after Christmas hits you, in January, February, and March, you say, "The Lord understands." You don't give and you say, "Things are going alright. We are getting a little out of debt." Suddenly, in April, May, and June you have a little accident here and there, but you are still hoping for a prosperous September.

When the harvest doesn't come in September, October, and November, you say, "Something's wrong, I wonder what's the matter? My finances are being attacked. The devil is a liar." No...it wasn't the devil, but you were the one responsible because you did not bring the right fragrance to Father when He asked for it. God is saying, "I want to give it to you, but you did not place any seed into the ground."

Trusting God for Your Harvest

"...I will not again curse the ground any more for man's sake..."

Genesis 8:21

The Bible has never advised you to trust man. The arms of flesh will fail you. When you become offended by what another individual has done, admit that you were looking for that individual to fulfill a need that only God can supply. Your trust is to only be in God. If you want to get disappointed quickly, start trusting man. You must lean on the Everlasting Arms.

Prophetic Principle #52

The Bible has never advised you to trust man.

Mark Twain said "If you help a dog to become prosperous that is starving, he won't bite you. But, if you help a man in the same condition, he will. That is the difference between a dog and a man."

The individual that you reach down and help the most is the individual who will turn on you the quickest. The individual that you seemingly do the least for will be the individual who will remain and endure until the end. If you don't learn some things through the Word of God, then experience will teach you. What the Word does not teach you, life will.

As long as there is a planet, the law of seedtime and harvest will remain. The law of seedtime and harvest means that we can see and know that there is a dependability of seasons. This is a God-given guarantee. When we sow seeds in the proper seasons, we will always reap a harvest.

Even if a farmer has a bad year, he doesn't reduce his sowing, he doubles his seed. Usually when you make a financial commitment to the work of the Lord, all of a sudden there is an attack launched to rob your harvest. At the point of attack, you should double your seed and prove the devil as a liar. If what you have presently financially is not meeting your need, you should plant all of your seed.

Before you become prosperous, you must first become prosperous in your mind. The architect first sees the plans for the structure in his mind before he goes out and builds the building. He then takes that which is on his mind and makes it a reality.

The Apostle John said, "Beloved, I wish above all things that thou mayest prosper and be in health, even as thy soul prospereth (3 John:2)." The prosperity of your outer man is always determined by the prosperity of your inner man. It does not begin from the outside and work its way inward, but from the inside and work its way outward. Your battle is in your mind. If you cannot see prosperity by faith, then you will not be prosperous. It must also be conceived before you can receive.

Prophetic Principle #53

Wealth finds all God-given ideas.

The harvest does not always come by walking outside the door and finding $200 at your feet, but it comes in wisdom and an idea. Wisdom will produce wealth if you use it properly. The difference between wealth and poverty is the ability to act in wisdom. Solomon understood that principle. He said wisdom is better than silver and gold.

Wealth finds all God-given ideas. Money is the easiest thing to replace. If you lose an arm, it is not easy to replace. If you lose a leg, it is not easy to replace. If you lose ten dollars, it is easy to replace. Father is no respecter of zeros. They don't make Him nervous.

I was in the Caribbean and some of those nations are the wealthiest nations in the world with their hidden resources. In Africa and certain parts of West Africa, there is a wealth of diamonds and gold, yet the people are the poorest. It is not because they don't have the resources, but the wisdom is not there to show how to draw them out.

Prophetic Principle #54

Money is the easiest thing to replace.

The Lord told me that He wanted the Church to be challenged in its understanding of the joy and the reality of giving. If you do not enter into the joy of giving, you will remain in the sacrifice of giving. He wants us to celebrate in our giving. To celebrate means "to honor or to observe."

God wants to take us from the sacrifice of a thing, such as praise, pray, and giving, to the place of operating in its joy. When we understand how to rejoice in that which God has given us, we will see an enormous difference in what the Father has ordained for us.

Chapter Eight
Eleven Reasons Why Men Fail

1. They lack the ability to organize details.

If you do not organize details, you are a candidate for failure. Is there any organization in your life? Are the shoes in your closet straightened up? Are your clothes straight? Is your room straight? Are things organized in your life?

2. They exercise no humility in their service.

When you humble yourself, God will exalt you.

3. When an individual expects pay for what they know, but not for what they can render.

The world pays for service, not for your knowledge. If knowledge created wealth, then every university professor would be a millionaire. The key to wealth is not in having head knowledge, but in your ability to apply the knowledge that you have obtained. How many of you know smart individuals who are poor? This is because they have not applied the knowledge that they have obtained.

4. **The fear of takeover will always keep you in a state of failure. You will eliminate your ability to duplicate or to mentor.**
   One manual said, "In order to get to where you need to go, you need three people to mentor you. In order for you to maintain a position, you need to be mentoring at least five other individuals. If you are not mentoring at least five individuals, that means that you are not going anywhere. Whatever position you get, you will not be able to maintain it because there is no cushion under the bottom to keep you where you need to be".

   Jesus did not spend much time with the multitude, He was busy pouring Himself into the disciples. If you are not pouring yourself into anyone, you are selfish. That is what salvation is all about. Jesus saved you so that you would go out and make disciples.

5. **Lack of imagination is another reason for failure. If you do not have the ability to use your mind to dream dreams, you will remain a failure.**
   One individual put it this way, "All individuals were born originals, but most people die copies".

6. **Disloyalty to those whom you serve and to those who serve you.**

Are you an individual of your word? Does your word have any meaning? If you do not believe that you can bring your own word to pass, you definitely will not believe that God can bring His word to pass. Do you want to know why God shows up late in your life? Because you show up late to places that you must go. If you show up early for events, God will show up early for events in your life.

Has it always seemed as though things in life have been a delayed reaction? Have you thought that maybe all you do is delay things in life. Don't forget that the law of seed time and harvest still works!

7. Procrastination. It is a thief of time.

Are you always waiting, scratching your head, afraid to take risks, afraid to go out on the limb? You want the fruit, but you are afraid to step out on the branch. If you fall, it is only a temporary defeat. Life is a risk. It is a risk every time you step out of your door, or just staying in your house.

8. A lack of persistence causes failure.

Some people give up too quickly. You do not lay into things long enough. You are quick to quit.

9. The lack of self control.

If your emotions get out of control you will not be successful, you are like a loose cannon. When your emotions get out of control, you can't think. That is why the devil keeps excitement in your life so that you can't think. Then he will have you beat.

If your sex life is out of control, you will be a failure. The Bible says a whore will bring a man to a piece of bread. You can build a mighty empire and all it takes is a lady to bring you to failure. You can have billions on the way to success, and all of a sudden the mystery of iniquity creeps in. Success is easy to attain, but takes more effort to maintain. When an individual has all that he needs to have, he begins to boast, "Well I have everything that is legal, maybe now I should try something that is illegal." It will bring you to a piece of bread.

10. Overcautiousness leads to failure.

If you get a case of the "what if's", you will never be an achiever or a winner.

11. Being in the wrong location.

Wrong location means "the wrong calling, the wrong line of work". If you do not love what you do, you will not be successful. Eighty percent of people are in jobs that they hate. If you just go to work for a paycheck, you will not be successful.

If you enter into a vocation which is actually your calling, you will work there if you earned ten dollars a week. Your financial resources will stretch. You will be empowered to create more substance.

When I worked for the Post Office making over $20,000 per year, with a one family income, God called me into the ministry. I had a love for the prophetic and the things of God. We started with 5 or 6 people. I preached to those few, yet we paid astronomical bills. I still do not know how they were paid. I believe that we had tapped into a law. God supernaturally brought the provision.

Money will only gravitate towards worthy causes, and will flee from non-worthy causes. If you do not have a cause at all, money will not come to you.

If you are intentionally dishonest, you will never be successful. You do not want to be an individual who gets on the phone disguising your voice or putting the answering machine on so that you can screen every call. What do you have to hide?

Prophetic Principle #55

Every idea is worth money.

These principles of success will take longer to obtain, but you will maintain your wealth. It won't come quickly, but it will endure. Some of you want the apple tree, but you want God to put the apples up there for you. God says take some years and plant some seed and let it pass through the hard place, then you will have a tree for life. You will have acquired something that can bear fruit every season, instead of waiting for something miraculous to happen each year.

21 Principles for Accumulating Wealth:

1. **You will always move towards your most dominant thought that is in your mind. If it is failure, you will move towards failure. If it is success, you will move towards it.**

2. **Riches always begin inside of a man, it never begins outside. It will have to start in the form of a thought. What are you thinking?**

3. You must give before you get. Every idea that you have can be turned into money, even if it is pet rocks. Someone had that idea and people bought it. Every idea is worth money.

4. Any desire you hold in your mind will eventually seek an expression of its own.

You have to be careful what you think about because one day it will break into action. That is why you can't have any room for hate. If you think, "I hate him, I am going to kill him," that thought will eventually express itself. You have to forgive and release. The enemy will use that and cause your anger to get out of control. You will sit there meditating upon that evil thought. Someone might say, "Can you hold my gun for me for the next couple of days?" It is then that your thought will seek expression.

5. True wealth will only last when it is based on truth and justice.

6. You must always have a definite aim. If not, you will not accumulate wealth. You must know where you are going.

7. Know the exact amount of money you want. If you do not have time to write it down, that means you do not have time to receive it.

8. Determine what you will do to generate the money. You must have a means whereby you can legally generate.

9. Establish a deadline for when you want the money to come in. If you do not put your pictures in frames, they can't hang.

10. Determine what you will give in exchange of money.

11. Your imagination is the place where plans and ideas evolve.

Casting down imaginations and everything that exalts itself against the knowledge of God. Your imagination is the thing that is used for plans and ideas. If you can dream it, you can have it. Anything the mind can conceive and believe, you will achieve.

It doesn't take an education to be successful. Many successful people were illiterate.

12. If you can imagine it, you can create it.

13. Poverty is attracted to the mind that is favorable to it.

14. Money is attracted to the minds that are prepared for it. Money has feelings.

15. You determine your own economic destiny. Some of you say, "I just left it all in His hands". The Lord says, "That is right, you just left it because I am sitting. I said "It is finished". Now you get up and do." Get off of your knees and onto your feet!

16. Money is shy; it must be wooed and pursued.

When I was interested in my wife, she was shy. I had to woo her and pursue her just like a man going after a woman whom he loves. Most men do not run after women who run after them. If she pursues him, he thinks that there must be something wrong. Money has to be attracted the same way. You have to do things to get it, just like you do some nice things to get the mate that you desire. You send some flowers. You ask her out to dinner. She may tell you no, but behind every no there is a yes. Sales people understand this principle.

17. You need faith, desire, and persistence in order for it to work.

18. Poverty and riches often exchange places.

When you get ready to dispossess poverty, then riches will come in, they always exchange places. They always meet one another in passing.

19. There is always a yes behind a no.

20. Defeat is a signal to try again. It is temporary.

21. Quitters never win and winners never quit.

When you can fight conformity, then you have the markings to become successful. It won't come without hard work. Also, understand that hard work will not make you wealthy. If that is the case, every factory worker should be a millionaire, and every slave should have been a multi-millionaire; they worked 12 and 14 hour days.

Prophetic Principle #56

Destiny is not left up to chance, but it's a matter of choice.

The key to success is using the tool which is the mind that God has given you. Let the ideas fall and watch what God will do with them. Ask God to give you the idea, and the ability to organize it and to make it work. Sometimes you can have too many ideas. You can become a jack of all trades and a master of none. I want you to concentrate on just one idea from start to finish. God wants to birth a dream in your life!

It's A Matter of Choice

Destiny is a matter of choice, it is not left up to chance. Chances don't determine your destiny, but choices do. Your life is not left up to chance, but it is a matter of choice. God placed in you a will. He gives you the ability to discern what His purpose is for your life.

It is not God's will that any should perish. Whatever the purpose of God is for your life will produce good fruit. God will not teach you how to lose, but He will show you how to profit. As you begin to walk in the principles of God's Kingdom, you will begin to walk in an understanding of God's Word. It is by being a doer of God's Word that you can be profitable; that is when the will of God will be a blessing.

You will not misinterpret the Word by saying that the sickness that you have is a part of the will of God for your life. You will not mistake the struggle that you are going through as God's will for your life. However, you will discern the purpose for your struggle, press forward, and learn to enjoy the season of your struggle. You will understand that every present struggle prepares you for a future achievement. Whatever hard place I find myself in, it is only bringing me to a place of preparation unto greatness.

Every seed has been ordained to be in the dark places of the earth. Even when a baby comes forth, it must push forth out of the darkness of a womb. Everything in life comes forth through a struggle. God has ordained the enemy or the adversary of your soul. He wants you to understand that for every seed of greatness that is within you, there is an equal seed of adversity that is assigned to you. The greater the blessing, the greater the testing.

Prophetic Principle #57

Your present struggle prepares you for tomorrow's achievement.

The higher you go up in God, the more principalities that are assigned to you to cause you to stumble. Your anointing will attract attack. That is why Jesus said you will receive a 100-fold return in this life, with persecution.

Don't think that you are going to get blessed and all of a sudden become devil-proof!! You will never graduate from opposition!! satan was walking along with Christ even up to the crucifixion. When you begin to rise in God, you will get to the place where not only God knows your name, but the devil will know your name. For some, the devil does not need to know their name because they are not doing anything to trouble his kingdom.

Some of us will never meet satan head on, for he has lesser ranking powers assigned to us. When you start disturbing nations, kingdoms, and ideologies, the devil himself will know your name. Satan is not omniscient nor is he omnipotent. He is not all-knowing nor all-powerful. He is not omnipresent; he cannot be at all places at all times. In our minds, however, we have given satan equal footing with God. But he is no match against God. All God has to do is say go and it is over.

If you do not like what state you are in today, all you have to do is change what you were doing yesterday. Today is the sum total of your yesterdays. Nevertheless, what you do today will be the sum total of your tomorrow.

BOOKS BY DR. E. BERNARD JORDAN

THE SCIENCE OF PROPH-ECY — A clear, concise and detailed exposition on the prophetic ministry and addresses many misnomers and misunderstandings concerning the ministry of the New Testament prophet. If you have any questions concerning prophetic ministry, or would like to receive sound, scriptural teachings on this subject, this book is for you! $6.95

MENTORING — THE MISSING LINK — Deals with the necessity of proper nurturing in the things of God by divinely appointed and anointed individuals placed in the lives of potential leaders. God's structure of authority and protocol for the purpose of the maturation of effective leadership is thoroughly discussed and explained. This book is highly recommended for anyone who believes that God has called them to any type of ministry in the Body of Christ. $6.95

PRAISE & WORSHIP — An extensive manual designed to give scriptural foundation to the ministry of the worshipping arts (musical, dramatic, artistic, literary, oratory, meditative and liturgical dance) in the House of the Lord. The arts are the outward mode of expression of an internal relationship with God, and are employed by God as an avenue through which He will speak and display His Word, and by man as a loving response to the touch of God upon his life. This book will compel the reader to deepen his relationship with his Creator, and explore new degrees of intimacy with our Lord and Saviour, Jesus Christ! $19.95

GIVING BIRTH TO PROPH-ECY is designed to help alleviate the various frustrations and miscarriages that occur when individuals receive the Word of the Lord in their lives. Many people are not aware of the power that is released when a prophetic word is spoken, and are unprepared for the various stages of development that they must pass through before they obtain the full manifestation of a prophecy that has come to pass. This book brings clarity in the midst of cloudiness, and offers a ready explanation for the various trials and testings that accompany the prophetic word. . .$6.95

MEDITATION: THE KEY TO NEW HORIZONS IN GOD is designed to help you unlock the inner dimensions of Scripture in your pursuit of the knowledge of God. Long considered exclusively in the domain of New Age and eastern religions, meditation is actually part of the heritage of Christians, and is to be an essential part of every believer's life. We have been given a mandate to meditate upon the Word of God in order to effect prosperity and wholeness in our lives. This book gives some foundational principles to stimulate our transformation into the express image of Jesus Christ.
. . . .$6.95

Tape Series by Dr. E. Bernard Jordan

The Making of the Dream — Are you riding the waves to an unknown shore? Is God's will passing you by? Is your God-given vision a dream or a reality? If you aren't sure of your life's destination, then you need to hear **The Making of the Dream!** These teachings are remarkable because they will assist you in establishing workable goals in pursuit of success. Your God-given dream will no longer be incomprehensible, but it will be touchable, believable and conceivable!
(4 tapes) $20.00

The Gatekeeper — Each person develops ''gatekeepers'' in their minds that will ascertain what will be received as acceptable truth and what will be received as a lie in the inner recesses of your mind. ''Gatekeepers'' must become subject to the Word of God, and those that embrace vain imaginations as truth must be cast down. This series teaches you to recognize the voice of a ''gatekeeper,'' and how to conquer it through the Word of God, thus allowing His truths to become the standard for our way of thinking.
(10 tapes) $45.00

Transference of Spirits — Deals with the impartation that occurs with the laying on of hands — its purposes, and the importance of leadership within a local body receiving the spirit of the leader. This series also discusses the difficulties that arise when there is a receptivity of a spirit contrary to that of the leader. Highly recommended for anyone that attends a local church.
(4 tapes) $20.00

School of the Prophets — Is there such a thing as ''The School of the Prophets'' today? What is its purpose? In these tapes, you will find a detailed definition, both scriptural and historical, of the necessity of the School of the Prophets and its function in the Body of Christ.
(4 tapes) $25.00

Dr. E. Bernard Jordan's
Zoe Ministries Video Library

The Joshua Generation — This video expounds the new militant army God is raising up in this hour, which will no longer peacefully coexist with the enemy. $27.50

School of the Prophets — This nine-tape video series is designed for those who would like to attend the School of the Prophets at home as a correspondence course. Includes a textbook and other materials, and a certificate upon completion. $495.00

Mentoring — An Art to Spiritual Protocol — This six-tape video series deals with the necessity of proper nurturing in the things of God by understanding authority and protocol......................$149.00

The Prophet and the Physician — Conversations with Dr. Jordan and Dr. Eric Womack, a naturepathic physician who clarifies the need in the Body of Christ for proper diet and exercise.................$27.50

Healing — In this video, Dr. Jordan interviews Vicki Jamison Peterson who has a profound healing ministry. Contains discussions on healing and its validity in the Body of Christ today.................$27.50

Plight of the Black Man in America — Conversations with Dr. Jordan and Leon Issac Kennedy. This video deals with the historic aspect of African Americans in the Pentecostal breakthrough at Azuza Street in the '20s to the present. $27.50

Money Is My Friend — Deals with the aspect of money in relation to the Kingdom of God. The Bible says, ''Make friends with unrighteous mammon.'' A must for those who want financial independence! $27.50

Prophecy to the Nations — During the Prophetic Conference, Powershift, Dr. Jordan prophesies regarding world events for the coming years. Powerful and enlightening! Recorded live. $27.50

Supernatural Provision of the Lord — Tape #2 in the money series. Deals with money, provision, and how giving corresponds to and determines your receiving the blessings of God. $27.50

UN Address/Power Shift '91 — This video was recorded live at the United Nations where Dr. Jordan was invited to speak concerning the nation of South Africa and the practice of Apartheid. $27.50

Men With Vision — Dr. Jordan speaks regarding the role of men in this hour in the Body of Christ. God is raising up men with vision who shall know God's plans and purposes as the sons of Issachar. $27.50

This is just a partial listing.
Call for complete catalog.
(718) 282-2014

ZOE MINISTRIES
4702 Farragut Road
Brooklyn, N.Y. 11203
(718) 282-2014

TO ORDER BY MAIL

NAME _____

ADDRESS _____

CITY _____ STATE _____

ZIP _____ PHONE ( ) _____

TO ORDER
BY CREDIT CARD
CALL NOW!
1-800-4 PROPHET

BOOKSTORES: Contact for volume discounts.

BOOKS/TAPES BY: Prophet/Teacher Bernard Jordan

QTY	TITLE	DONATION	TOTAL

GUARANTEE:
You may return any defective item within 90 days for replacement. All offers are subject to change without notice. Please allow 4 weeks for delivery.

No COD Orders Accepted

Make checks payable to:
ZOE MINISTRIES

Subtotal	
Shipping	
Offering	
TOTAL	

I WOULD LIKE FURTHER INFORMATION ON (CHECK AREA OF INTEREST):

- [ ] School Of The Prophets
- [ ] Tape Catalog/Mailing List
- [ ] Special Conferences/Activities

Shipping

Order	U.S.	Foreign
$1-20	$3.00	12%
$21-60	$4.00	of
$61-100	$5.00	Gross
$101-up	7%	

New Release From
Dr. E. Bernard Jordan!!
By Popular Demand . . .

Mentoring — "An Art To Spiritual Protocol"

In addition to our workbook Spiritual Protocol, we now have created a new video teaching series for Spiritual Protocol. This is a six tape series expounding on the principles of divine structure and order in the House of the Lord. A must for all ministerial staff and laypersons alike!

Special Introductory Price

$149.95

ORDER TODAY!

Name _____

Address _____

City _____ State _____ Zip _____

Please make checks payable to ZOE MINISTRIES
☐ M/C   ☐ Visa   ☐ Discover   ☐ American Express

Card No. _____ Exp. Date_____

Signature _____ Amt. Enclosed $_____

Please add additional $4.00 for postage and handling.